Spiritual Guidance for the Separated and Divorced

Medard Laz

LIGUORI
PUBLICATIONS

One Liguori Drive
Liguori, Missouri 63057
(314) 464-2500

Imprimi Potest:
John F. Dowd, C.SS.R.
Provincial, St. Louis Province
Redemptorist Fathers

Imprimatur:
Monsignor Edward J. O'Donnell
Vicar General, Archdiocese of St. Louis

ISBN 0-89243-158-X

Copyright © 1982, Liguori Publications
Printed in U.S.A.

Cover Design: P. Hummelsheim

The LORD is my light and my salvation;
    whom should I fear?
Hear, O LORD the sound of my call;
    have pity on me, and answer me.
Wait for the LORD with courage;
    be stouthearted, and wait for the LORD.

Psalm 27:1,7,14

Contents

Introduction

The last ten years have produced an abundance of self-help books to assist the numerous people whose marriages have ended in separation and divorce. My own *Helps for the Separated and Divorced, Learning to Trust Again* (Liguori Publications) was written to aid these men and women as they passed through grief and guilt and to encourage them to trust again as a new life was dawning.

Beyond the search for emotional and psychological growth, there is a great need for a spiritual and prayerful journey for those who have experienced one of the greatest modern day tragedies — the death of a marriage.

Each chapter of this booklet begins with the thoughts and feelings of different individuals who are now trying to relate to the circumstances brought on by separation and divorce. Then follows a short reflection or prayer. It is my fond hope that these experiences and prayers will provide spiritual healing and increase the love of God in the life of each reader. You are not alone in your journey from death to resurrection. The Lord is with you!

I extend my sincerest appreciation to all those who are separated and divorced, especially those who are a part of The Beginning Experience. Because they have opened their lives to me, I have been better able to fathom the Spirit of the Almighty who dwells so wondrously deep within the human heart.

Medard Laz

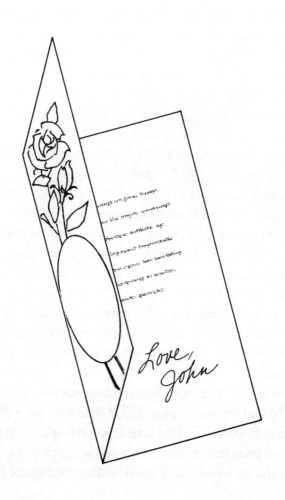

1
"What Will It Cost?"

One day I was in a gift shop to purchase a birthday card for a friend. As I scanned the selections, I noticed a short, stocky man, at least in his sixties, standing next to me. He was surveying the birthday cards displayed under the heading "Wife." With each card he did something most unusual. He would pick out one, glance at the front, and immediately flip it over to check out the price on the back. He did this repeatedly, sometimes staring at the front and then the inside, looking for proof that it was worth seventy-five cents or a dollar.

The longer I watched the man, the more upset I became. "What difference does it make?" I kept asking myself. What was an extra quarter or fifty cents? My God, he looked like he had been married for forty years or more. I wanted to jab him and say, "You ought to be happy that you have a wife whose birthday you can celebrate. I'm half your age, and I no longer have a mate. Why are you so worried about the price?"

I bought my card and left the store. I had not said anything to the man, but the scene stayed vividly with me. I was still seething inside. "How could a man be so cheap, especially when he still has his spouse?"

As I drove off, my thoughts took a turn. I began to think of myself and how *I* approach other people. The more I reflected, the more I realized that *I was no different* than the man I had just left. The first question that comes to my mind before giving of myself to another is: *"What will it cost?"* I don't like to admit it, but this question was always on my subconscious mind as my marriage was ending. Rarely was I ever willing to give myself unconditionally to my spouse or to anyone, even my children. Even today, before I offer to take the kids to the zoo or a carnival, I still inquire within: "What will it cost?" I never say "yes" to a meeting or a committee without first asking myself: "What will it cost?" I used to think that cost meant dollars and cents. Today I realize that it has nothing to do with money.

I differ little from the man who unsettled me in the gift shop. I don't really want to trust or to give myself. I don't want to risk loving and then not be appreciated for myself in the end. I could not stand getting hurt again after all the pain I have been through because of my divorce.

Reflection

Lord Jesus, unlike me, you never asked the question, *"What will it cost?"* You came to pay the *full* price of our redemption, even to a bloody death on a cross. You paid the price when, as tired as you were after a long, hot day, you ignored the overanxiety of your disciples and said: "Let the children come to me and do not hinder them. It is to just such as these that the kingdom of God belongs'' (Mark 10:14). You never backed away. You always came forward — to the troubled centurion, the widowed mother, and the wavering apostles.

How frustrated and terminally alone you were that Thursday night in the Garden when you spoke to your disciples: ''My heart is nearly broken with sorrow. Remain here and stay awake with me.'' And when you returned to find them asleep: ''So you could not stay awake with me for even an hour?'' (Matthew 26:38,40) You asked very little from your disciples, Jesus — just an hour — and they would not give it. In my own small way, I think I know how you felt. I've looked to friends for an hour of care and support, and they would not give it. And, on the other hand, they have sought my attention for five minutes, and I have been so wrapped up in myself that I did not even hear their plea.

Lord, your life, your death, your presence with me today has taught me that love has no price tag. Love cannot be bought or sold in a gift shop or at the candy counter. It can only be given away upon a cross. I see now that the more of my love I give away, the more love I will receive in return.

2
"Is That All There Is?"

One of my favorite songsters of the not-so-distant past is a singer by the name of Peggy Lee. I remember being immensely impressed by one of her songs that asked the question, "Is that all there is?" The theme revolved around the idea that if there is no tomorrow, we might as well live it up today. Those lyrics have floated through my head many times. I keep on telling myself that there must be more to life than just today. Yet, after my divorce, I have felt that there is little or no life left for me in this world. I keep wondering, "If that's all there is, then what's the use?"

I suppose that I have always been on a continual search for perfection. I have never found it, and that is why I get so frustrated. God made the world and all of its creatures imperfect. He had to for he alone is perfect. The last place for me to look for perfection is in myself; and the second last place is in my former spouse, who is no more perfect than I am. Why should I expect perfection in mere creatures when God never intended it? Even Adam and Eve had their problems. And, no doubt, that's why I'm having them too. I have love in my heart, but so much of it has evaporated that there are few family members and friends that I can refresh.

Because I am not perfect does not mean that I am no good. Rather, it means that I am very good. Even with — and in spite of — all my imperfections I can still be loved. I cannot bury them or hide them; I can only accept them and grow beyond them. The very fact that I ask the question, "Is that all there is?" convinces me that there is a whole lot more to my life.

Reflection

Heavenly Father, there just has to be more, an infinite amount more to my world. Rather than create just one rose, you fashioned a worldwide garden of roses, to be admired, picked, smelled, and enjoyed. You did not stop with the creation of one man and one woman; you breathed life into a universal family, so that no one of us would ever be far from your love and your presence. The only time I ask: "Is that all there is?" is when I have closed my eyes and my life to you and plunged myself into my own private, inner darkness. For you have fixed not just one sun in the sky, Lord; you have showered this globe with billions of suns, one for each of us to have, to hold, and to share.

I'll never be eternally happy on this planet, Lord. For no one and no thing can give me more than fleeting joy. That is why your Son calls me to look beyond today and tomorrow and to gaze at forever.

All that I desire in life is to add to the goodness and joy that you have placed deep within me from the moment of my conception. For beneath my flesh and blood is a well-spring of your abiding love.

If there is life after death, and I believe that there is, then there is life after divorce. I believe in life — life after death and life after divorce. You, Lord, are that life.

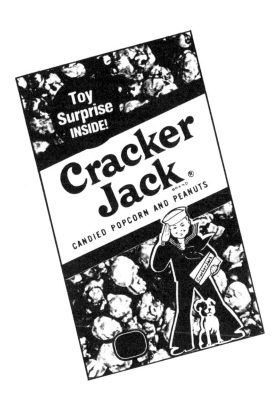

3
"Where Is My Prize?"

I tend to handle my life in the same way that I handle a box of Cracker Jack. I have always been attracted to this particular confection. Why? I can't wait to get to the "prize in every box." I like to see what I have won. The instructions plainly say to open the box at the top. Nevertheless, I follow my own instincts and always open the box at the bottom. I'm in such a hurry to get to the prize. I push aside the popcorn and the nuts in order to discover what I have won. I always like to be a winner.

What did I win? Where is my prize? These are the questions I have always asked. When I got married it was like winning what I had wanted forever — someone to love and someone to love me in return. The one I married was my prize.

But during the marriage I didn't follow the instructions. I went at it from the wrong end, just like I do with a box of Cracker Jack. I was so obsessed with seeking the prize — a beautiful home, unrestricted time alone with my spouse — that I was unwilling to spend my time in the sharing and caressing and dialoging so necessary to attain the prize. As with a box of Cracker Jack, I all too frequently turned my marriage over and went at it the wrong way. I knew what *I* wanted, but I rarely took the time to appreciate what *we* wanted.

Reflection

Lord, your words have turned the world upside down. In the past it was always "an eye for an eye and a tooth for a tooth." And today so many people say: "Get away with anything you can." "The first law is survival." But you said, "Turn the other cheek . . . Walk the extra mile . . . Forgive seven times seventy times . . . When someone takes your coat, let him have your shirt as well." And you confirmed all this with the words: "Love one another as I have loved you" (John 15:12).

Jesus, you have turned my world upside down. Getting a divorce was like having a heart attack and not going to the hospital. It has made me so different. People tell me that I have a new glow, a sparkle, that they have never seen before. I should tell them that it is all because I have let you into my life.

Once you said: "My mother and my brothers are those who hear the word of God and act upon it" (Luke 8:21). I have heard your words, dear Lord, and I am trying — oh, how I am trying — to walk the extra mile by going to counseling, to forgive seven times seventy phones and doors being slammed on me, and to hand over my shirt, as well as my coat, by making the child support payments promptly.

Lord, you are my prize. I thank you for your patient waiting.

4
"Why Am I a Mother?"

One day my three-year-old son, Billy, returned home from playing with his friends. I asked him what he had been up to all afternoon. "Oh, not much, Mom, I only committed adultery." I nearly choked on the grape that I was eating.

"Billy, how can you say a thing like that? Do you know what adultery means?"

"Sure, Mom," smiled Billy innocently, "adultery means doing what adults do."

Reflection

Lord, I often wonder why *I*, of all people, was chosen to be a mother? Those first few months — after "we knew" and I began "to show" — were wonderful. And I will never forget that first "flutter," assuring me that my baby was alive. That last month of waiting, however, found me fluctuating between joy — at what was about to happen — and anxiety — that something might go wrong.

So soon the time of waiting was no more — a hurried ride to the hospital; the time in the labor room; and then that exquisite moment when I was able to tell the whole world that I had given birth to a child. What a privilege — for a husband and wife to cooperate with almighty God in bringing new life into the world, a life destined for some years here on earth, a life meant for an eternity in heaven.

Only a mother knows the ecstasy of holding total helplessness in her own arms. No one other than a mother can experience the sensation of seeing her child's eyes open for the very first time, of blowing gently into the delicate ears, of marveling at the mouth that could yawn so wide, of tracing the perfect slope of the nose, of caressing the hair as soft as down, of stroking the tiny toes and fingers so round and so soft. I could never grow tired of doing all these things over and over again, for I had helped you, Lord, to create a human person. How I relished and enjoyed the baby that clung to my breast.

But why did you choose *me* to be a mother? This question has haunted me through the years. Slowly, I have had to melt away my own selfishness, my first concern being for my child. My life has been centered around the sleeping innocence of my firstborn. I have had to offer more than even midnight hours to still the outbreak of tears. And, as my child grew older, with each cut knee I was cut, with each broken balloon I became deflated, and with each lost game I lost my own self.

Then came the time when I had to give my child away — to teachers with whom I did not always agree, to playmates of whom I did not always approve, and finally to a weekend father who tries to buy love on a merry-go-round or at the hobby shop.

As a mother, I want to protect and shield — even take all the blows myself — but I know that I must allow my child to grow. When mothering becomes smothering there is no chance for growth on the part of a child.

Helplessly and without a husband, dear Lord, I have had to watch my child adopt ways and develop habits that defy my many hours of patient and loving training. All this hurts me so very deeply. But never — other than to you, Lord — have I uttered a single word of my vexation to anyone. Alone in my bed these last few years, I have survived on my late-night prayers. Thank you for staying up late to listen. Lord, no matter how big, how sassy, how married and faraway Billy is, I'll always still long to hold that *baby* in my arms.

5
"Why Am I a Father?"

They wheeled me out of my room and down the hall toward the elevator. My body and my mind were numb. My heart was pounding like an air hammer at a construction site. I was totally helpless. For the next few hours my life would be completely in the hands of my doctor. I was headed for open-heart surgery.

My daughter was beside me every step of the way, her eyes streaming with tears. "Good luck, Dad. I'll be praying for you. Oh, Dad, I love you!" I tried to answer her, but my tongue was too dry to form the words. For over twenty years I had strained to say those three words, "I love you," but they just would not come.

The elevator doors slammed shut, separating the two of us for what would seem to be an eternity. At the very moment when I most wanted to say "I love you," I was unable to do so.

Reflection

Lord, I often wonder why *I,* of all people, was chosen to be a father? I remember asking myself this as I gently placed my hand on my wife's stomach, waiting anxiously to feel the "flutter" of new life. Would it be a boy named after me or the longed-for little girl who would put her arms around my neck and hug me for a lifetime?

Nervously, I waited. Would I hold the baby gently enough? (I had never been one to display open affection.) Would I live up to the promises I had made to myself and to you when my wife told me she was pregnant? Could I provide the clothes, the food, and the money for college? Would I stop smoking so that this new life could breathe unpolluted air? Would I be able to furnish the good example so important for every father to give? Most of all, would I manifest the love that he or she needed from me?

That first time I held my baby daughter in my arms, dear Lord, I realized somehow why after each act of creation you looked and "found it very good." I never wanted to let go of holding her! All little girls are wonderful, but this one was very special — so helpless, so beautiful, so mine. But even that very first day I could not bring myself to say — "I love you." Why did you choose *me* to be a father?

Later in our marriage, when my wife and I quarreled violently and I took to drinking excessively, I finally moved out. It was then that I wanted to turn in my fatherhood — like a criminal turning himself in to the police. I didn't. Rather, I blamed her mother, and I made my daughter feel like a burden rather than the joy that she has always been.

When I finally left home, I was not sure whether my daughter ever wanted to see me again. I know that she disapproved of my new life-style and my reasons for the divorce. But she did want to spend time with me, and when I took her to dinner on occasion, she dressed like a princess and treated me like a king. So why could I not put "I love you" into words? It is too simple to say that my parents never said it to me. I've never been one for laying the blame, Lord.

My daughter has been the one constant, bright spot in my life. She always greets me with, "Hi, Dad, how are you doing?"

Dear Jesus, you turned water into wine at Cana, and you lit my heart of stone into a glowing coal at my daughter's wedding. Somehow I even doubted that she would ask me to walk her down the aisle. But after I did and I took back her veil and kissed her, the miracle of my life happened. *"I love you!"* The words finally came to my lips. Good God, now I know why you chose *me* to be a father. Not a day has gone by since the wedding that I have not called her up, sometimes to say nothing more than — *"I love you!"*

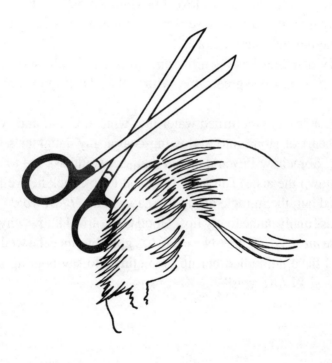

6
My Right Side

I was out of town on business for an extended period, and as time went on I became more aware of the extreme length and untidy appearance of my hair. My hometown barber always cut my hair just the way I liked it, but I knew I could not wait until I returned home for my next haircut.

On my first free afternoon, I headed for the nearest barber-shop. Once in the chair, I watched carefully — in the facing mirror — each snip of the scissors. I was delighted to see the meticulous job the new barber was performing.

After some time he walked around in front of the chair and spoke to me seriously: "There is something I must tell you about your head." Horrible thoughts flashed through my mind. "Was I going bald?" "Had he found a lump?"

My response was a stutter, "Wha . . . what's the matter?"

"Have you always parted your hair on the left side of your head?" he inquired.

"Yes, of course," I answered.

"Well, you've been parting it on the *wrong* side of your head. Your crown is on the *right* side."

I have always felt that there was something wrong with me. Before our divorce, especially during the final months of our marriage, I could never measure up to my spouse's expectations. No matter what I did or said, it was wrong. Life had become one big put-down.

I thought that I knew myself pretty well, but I didn't. I came apart at the seams. I never thought of myself as a violent person, yet I was becoming a monster around the house. I started disliking myself even more.

But now I am beginning to realize my strength. I am learning to absorb criticism. I am adjusting to eating, sleeping, and watching TV alone. Formerly, I felt that I was the weak one in the marriage. Now I realize that I was really the strong one. I may not have been vocal or pushy, but day in and day out, I did keep things together.

Reflection

I bless the LORD who counsels me;
   even in the night my heart exhorts me.
I set the LORD ever before me;
   with him at my right hand I shall not be disturbed.
Therefore my heart is glad and my soul rejoices,
   my body, too, abides in confidence;
Because you will not abandon my soul to the nether world,
   nor will you suffer your faithful one to undergo corruption.

You will show me the path to life,
  fullness of joys in your presence,
  the delights at your right hand forever.

Psalm 16:7-11

Dear Lord, I thought that I knew you. But I had pigeonholed you for Sunday mornings in the time slot before I read the morning paper. The only other time I recognized you was when I was in trouble.

It's not Sunday morning, and I'm no more in trouble right now than I have been in for months. That is why I am praying to you from my heart. Lord, you don't see sides or take sides — of my head or of my divorce. All you see and all that I want you to take is my heart.

7
My Greatest Fear

Your old men shall dream dreams,
   your young men shall see visions.

Joel 3:1

(But how about the rest of us?)

My greatest fear in life is not that someday I may die of cancer. What I fear most of all is waking up some morning and discovering that I died years ago and didn't even know it. To just go through the physical motion of living when the inner life has already died is a fate more cruel than physical death.

Reflection

I am not looking for perfect happiness in this world, dear Lord. Contentment most of the time would do. Now that I'm divorced, I'm searching for a new me, not born of bitterness or malcontent, but a new me who belongs. I can hardly remember my new street address, but I belong there because I've got so much to give where I live now.

After my divorce I made a decision to live — to get up each morning and to look up above the clouds, to grow flowers and to give flowers, to shed tears and to wipe them from others' faces, to enjoy the stars and to pass their twinkle on to others.

I've made cloudy days bright, and I will again. I've rescued fallen ones and mended broken wings, and I will again. I've influenced countless friends and strangers to start humming and whistling and singing, and I will again.

You knew well that I'd have my problems with today, Lord, and that is why you blessed me with tomorrow.

> Lord, make me an instrument of your peace,
>> Where there is hatred, let me sow love.
>> Where there is injury, let me sow pardon.
>> Where there is doubt, to sow faith.
>> Where there is despair, to sow hope.
>> Where there is darkness, to sow light.
>> And where there is sadness, let me sow joy.
> O Divine Master,
>> Grant that I may not so much seek
>>> To be consoled as to console,
>>> To be understood as to understand,
>>> To be loved as to love.
>> For it is in giving that we receive.
>> It is in pardoning that we are pardoned.
>> And it is in dying that we are born to eternal life.
>>> *(St. Francis of Assisi)*

8
Running for Life

The greatest sporting event that I have ever witnessed was not a World Series or a Super Bowl or a Kentucky Derby, but a Special Olympics event for the physically handicapped.

It was a hundred-yard dash for ten teenaged boys and girls. The gun sounded, and they all headed up the track. Soon after the start one of the boys stumbled and fell. The other nine runners immediately stopped and converged on the fallen young man. Then, together, they helped him get back on his feet. Once that was done, the Special Olympics race continued.

Many people pretend that running is living. For them, it is the "great escape." After my divorce I became a master of the "great escape." But real living consists of recognizing one's own handicaps and in being courageous enough to stoop down and help others who are handicapped.

"There is no greater love than this: to lay down one's life for one's friends" (John 15:13).

Reflection

Dear Jesus, life is not a problem, a struggle, or a race. Life is a family. We all have our foibles. We all fail and fall. Every one of us needs help to rise again. We all belong to the same fallen family.

Jesus, as you bled to death on the Cross, you said to your mother, Mary: "Woman, there is your son," and to your beloved John, "There is your mother" (John 19:26-27). Lord, Mary was *your* mother. And John was no more her son than I.

You knew that John needed a mother and that Mary needed a son. So in your one last act before you died, you brought the two of them together as a family. You have the same desire for me today.

I'm no longer a married person, but I am a family person who needs to stop running. Instead of trying to escape to Mars, I can be a friend who lays down his life, who stops to help a child, a stranger, a fellow handicapped, and yes, at times, even my former spouse. Send anyone you wish, Lord. We are all a part of the human family.

Dear Lord, this is why you make today a new day — so that each of us can help each other and begin anew each morning.

9

Too Close to See

I had always wanted to see a "Monday Night Football" game in person. One year my calendar was clear, and so I purchased two tickets for a friend and myself. At the ticket office I asked: "Are these good seats?" "You'll be very close to the action" was the reply.

When we arrived at the stadium, I approached three ushers to help me find the seats. None of them had any idea of where my section was located. Finally, one usher told me that these were portable seats set up right at the edge of the playing field. We went down and took our places. The view was great; we were right on the fifty-yard line. We would be part of the action.

But when the sidelines filled up with the massive hulks of football players and the game began, we could see nothing of what was happening on the field just a few yards in front of us. The players on the sidelines could move with the action of each play, but we had to stay in our seats. We could not see anything because we were *too close!*

Reflection

Lord, this has been my problem with life. I've stayed too close to the action. I have not taken the time to step back and reflect, to get a better view of what was happening.

Because I was so close to the battlefront during my separation and divorce, I lost perspective. I ended up hating the one person I was supposed to love. The kids have become third class citizens, at best. I've reached for aspirins and sleeping pills and alcohol to deaden the pain. Many a night I have crawled into bed and hoped that I would not wake in the morning. Every sunrise has immediately given way to a sunset, since every new day has only meant a whole new set of worries.

But now that I have stepped back to take a better look, I notice the miracles that you have been working, Lord. The kids have settled down; my former spouse is into counseling (as am I); and I've received a raise at work. Having finally gotten up on my own two feet and taken a stand, I'm back visiting with you regularly at church; and I'm even helping a fellow worker who suffered nearsightedness similar to mine.

There is an old adage, dear Lord, that says you never give people more than they can handle. My life immediately before and after my divorce made me doubt the truth of that statement. But now I see what the words mean. You didn't give me too much to handle. I just didn't find the right handle until I changed from *my* handle to *yours*.

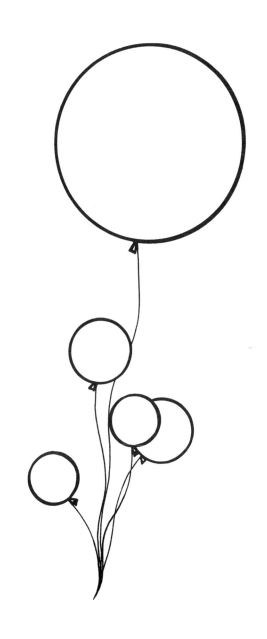

10
Me and My Balloon

I was four years old when my parents took me to a state fair one summer. After enjoying the rides, I pleaded with Mom and Dad to buy me one of the helium-filled balloons being sold by a vendor. A dollar was a lot of money back then, and it took more than a few of my tears to convince my parents.

Riding home on the train, my spirits were as high as my balloon. I felt like I had found a new playmate. I couldn't wait to get home to play with and talk to my friendly balloon.

Ever so proudly I walked down our street, holding on tightly to the string. I listened with delight as the kids on the block whistled and exclaimed: "Oh look!"

On my arrival home, I took one step into the house and a wooden sliver on the doorway suddenly popped my pretty balloon. My tears and my screams were a torrent of agony and disbelief. No amount of comforting by my parents would ease my pain — not even when they said they would buy me another balloon. But I knew it would never be the same.

Reflection

That was many years ago, Lord. I've had many popped balloons since then. Every time that I say "No" to you and to your love, I spoil the happiness that you want me to have. "No, I'm too busy to spend time with the kids." "No, I don't want to know about your troubles; I have enough of my own." "No, I just want to be left alone."

That last excuse, Lord, is untrue. "I *don't* want to be left alone." I'm too alone. I dread going home after work. That's why I stop for a drink. I detest weekends without the kids, so I keep on the go. My house is not a home anymore. It seems that the old house died along with my divorce.

But now, Lord, I'm learning to be alone. I've stopped drowning my sorrows with drink. I no longer pester my friends with insistent telephone calls. You went into the desert to be alone — not to run away but to get a feel for life. Before every major decision — as you began your public life, chose your disciples, journeyed to Jerusalem for the last time — you went off by yourself to pray. You needed to be alone.

Alone, I'm beginning to savor life, to enjoy who I am. In the past, life always meant doing something exciting or being with someone. It's nice to be responsible just for myself. Thank you for letting me know that I'm never really alone when I'm with you. Life is much more rewarding now that I am blowing up balloons rather than popping them.

11
Letting Go

When I was five years old I was taken to the hospital to have my tonsils removed. Already scared to death, I received no help from my two older brothers. They told me that the ice cream served that first night was not regular ice cream, but that it had medicine in it. So the night before my surgery I lay back, my cheeks streaming with tears, as a huge mound of ice cream melted before my eyes.

I remember my fright as I was strapped down on a table and wheeled into the operating room. At that time ether was used, and I recall the mask coming down on my face. Wanting to take one more big breath, I screamed out, "Wait! Wait!" But I was fast asleep.

Reflection

Lord, it has always been hard for me to let go. I hold on for dear life — to the car's steering wheel when I'm on an icy road, to my child's hand when walking across a street, to a dividend check that arrives in the mail.

During my divorce proceedings, I kept crying out, "Wait! Wait!" I did not want to let go of a spouse I had vowed to love, my modest home, the unfinished business of married life, the promises of tomorrow, and the little security that I had.

Finally, Lord, I uttered your prayer in the Garden: "Father, if it is your will, take this cup from me; yet not my will but yours be done" (Luke 22:42).

I had given the marriage my all. I had consulted everyone that I could, sobbing through boxes and boxes of tissues, but nothing I did seemed to help. I didn't want the divorce. Despite all my work and worry, it was simply inevitable, like the last chapter in a book. This cup of tragedy could not pass me by without my drinking it.

Dear Lord, your will concerning my marriage remains hidden; but I do know that you want me to be alive, to go on living. Your coming back to life after dying on the Cross is my hope for the future. In so many ways I'll always carry the cross of my divorce, but I'm beginning to look beyond it to a new life.

As a child I believed my brothers about the medicine in the ice cream. I trusted my spouse about our marriage. Trust, faith, hope, belief, tomorrow — there is no other way to live, even if on occasion it means dying to myself.

Lord, thanks for waiting for me to let go. I place myself in your hands. "Not my will but yours be done."

12
?,.!

Reflection

My life, O Lord, resembles a procession of punctuations: a question mark here, a comma, a period, an exclamation point there.

At times my head is a whirlwind of questions: Why me? Why does everything always happen to me? How will I survive? Why was I so naïve? When will my life ever settle down? Most of the time there are no adequate answers to the majority of these questions. I envision my life as a series of problems to be solved.

At other times, my heart beats out a string of commas. Commas drag things out. Divorce has made my life seem like a revolving millstone of work, rest, eat, play, and sleep, with a heavy emphasis on work.

More than anyone else, dear Lord, you know that question marks and commas have become a way of life for me after my divorce. There is so little lasting peace or joy in my life.

But I thank you now, Lord, for helping me to reach a period in my life when I can close things off. A period makes an ending: maybe a happy one, maybe a sad one, but an ending nonetheless. I need periods in my life so that I can find my new beginnings.

What I am really searching for is an exclamation point! This is my dream and my goal. I want to be alive to celebrate who I am and all that is precious in my life. I will continue to reach for the exclamation point so that I can enjoy every nonrepeatable moment to the fullest.

Heavenly Father, my exclamation points affirm everyone in my life and you, the believable God who made me. I need your love and your exclamation points!

13
A Person of Few Words

I am a person of few words:
    "Who knows?"
    "We'll see, we'll see."
    "Shut your mouth."
    "I'm busy!"
    "I'll show you."
    "Get out!"
    "Please!"
    "No!"
    "The kids, the kids."
    "Later."

Reflection

Jesus, too, is a person of few words:

"Be not afraid."

"Your sins are forgiven."

"Come, follow me."

"Love one another."

"Take up your cross."

"Bear witness."

"Weep not for me."

"Watch and pray."

"Feed my lambs."

"Peace!"

14
"Hey! Man on the Cross"

"Hey! Man on the Cross, why are you still hanging there? Do you want to be taken down?" Two thousand years . . . your arms must be weary, your legs must be stiff, and your heart — your heart must be broken.

"Hey! Man on the Cross, do you know what's happening?" Some churches have taken you down, but not for the right reason. A crucified Savior does not appeal to their congregations. And to many people you are just a museum piece.

Oh, what you did needed doing. But all of that was so very long ago, they say. People dressed, acted, and spoke differently then. This is the space age — the era of television, trips to the moon and to faraway planets. In this streamlined world you are no longer thought to be in the mainstream.

I'm so disgusted, weary, and depressed. It has been a long time since I was pleasant with anyone. I'm exhausted. My so-called friends — they don't really pay attention to me. The boss — he's always trying to kill me with work. The neighbors — they're a disgrace with their constant bickering. No one in the world has time for me. All that the world thinks about is the world.

Is it any wonder that many marriages are breaking up? I'm no longer surprised that mine came to an end. So many people take drink after drink, tranquilizer after tranquilizer. Broken windows, shattered hearts, lying lips, savage slaughter. What is the matter with people? Don't they ever pause for a moment and see you still hanging there?

Reflection

Hey! Man on the Cross, I just noticed how naked you are. This is such a cold day. Here, take my coat. It's all right. I'm a survivor. You mentioned how thirsty you are. Here, take this drink. I seem to always have more than enough to drink. Those thorns on your head — they must hurt. Let me take them from you. It's OK. My hands are calloused from all of the rough jobs I've had. I wish that there was more that I could do. Your disciples and friends are beside themselves with grief. As soon as I leave here I will go and comfort them.

But before I run, Man on the Cross, there is something I must tell you. You have hung there for a long, long time, and I thank you for that. If it weren't for your hanging there, I would never have been able to hang on here.

15
"I'm Sorry"

One day I decided to try my hand at artificial flower arrangements. I went to a large department store to buy the kind of silk flowers I would need. While making my selections, I noticed a display of eucalyptus branches. They smelled delightful, and the burnt-red color looked stunning in a magnificent white vase.

Trying to get a better look at the branches, I inadvertently caused the vase to topple from its shelf. I caught my breath — but, unfortunately, not the vase — and within a split second dozens of white fragments were strewn at my feet.

A young saleswoman hurried over. I was immensely embarrassed.

"I'm sorry — I'm so terribly sorry," I said.

"It's all right, it's all right," she said to soothe my feelings.

"No, it's not all right," I retorted, "I was careless. How much was the vase? Let me pay for it."

"Don't be silly," she said. "One of the women in gift wrapping dropped a five hundred dollar vase just yesterday. That will be taken care of, and so will your accident. We're *insured*."

People take out insurance for so many things — the house, the furniture, the car, their lives — and they can even arrange for compensation in case they lose their jobs. But I had no insurance to protect me from the breakup of my marriage. My spouse and I had to pick up the pieces individually.

Once I had an automobile accident, but the person whose car was damaged seemed more interested in getting his car repaired than in hearing me say "I'm sorry." Divorce is not like a car accident. There is no insurance to pay for the damages. That is why expressing sorrow is so very important.

During my marriage I'm afraid I worried only about placing blame: "You've never met my needs . . . You don't understand . . . You can't be trusted . . . You won't help yourself . . . You've hurt the kids terribly." But I have to accept my part of the blame for our marriage breakup. Most of all I need to say "I'm sorry," and at the same time be ready to forgive.

Reflection

Father, forgive them; they do not know what they are doing.
Luke 3:34

Jesus, how true those words of yours from the Cross! And my divorce calls them vividly to mind. So much of what my spouse and I did needed mutual forgiveness, because we really didn't know what we were saying or doing. How could it all end this way? I'll never figure it out. Love should never end on a cross — for you or for us — but it does.

That is why on the Cross you asked the Father to forgive, why you ask me to say "I'm sorry." Those words can heal the real hurts of life. A doctor's words, "Results are negative," do not heal. A beloved's words, "I love you," do not heal. But when I, offender that I am, say "I'm sorry," the road to recovery of inner peace and healing has begun.

You know very well, Jesus, that there is no insurance for the human heart to prevent it from being broken. That is why you came down from heaven and, like no prophet before you in history, you showed us that love does mean saying "I'm sorry."

16
"Thank You, God!"

Once upon a time there was a giant who lived near the top of a high mountain. Every morning he would climb to the top and fill the valley below with the roar of his anger and his insults.

Across the valley — on an equally high mountain — lived another giant. Every morning he was roused from his sleep by the noise from across the valley. So he would stalk to the top of his mountain and howl back at the other giant.

On one such occasion, a tiny worm down in the valley poked his head up from the earth and saw how brightly the sun was shining. And, despite all the noise from above, the worm was heard to say: "Thank you, God, for such a beautiful day."

Reflection

Dear Lord, at one point during my marriage I made up my mind that I would never become bitter or filled with hatred. Yet, so often I would wake up angry, and everyone around me sensed it. And eventually I found myself hating the one I was supposed to love — the person I married.

For so long the two of us were like those two giants — rude and ill-tempered. We would take our positions at the tops of our separate mountains to shout at each other, forgetting our kids, our responsibilities, and our own self-worth. But now, Lord, I'm tired of trying to survive on bitterness.

The LORD is my shepherd; I shall not want.
    In verdant pastures he gives me repose;
Beside restful waters he leads me;
    he refreshes my soul.
He guides me in right paths
    for his name's sake.
Even though I walk in the dark valley
    I fear no evil; for you are at my side
With your rod and your staff
    that give me courage.
You spread the table before me
    in the sight of my foes;
You anoint my head with oil;
    my cup overflows.
Only goodness and kindness follow me
    all the days of my life;
And I shall dwell in the house of the LORD
    for years to come.

Psalm 23

Thank you, Lord, for leading me down from my mountain of animosity into the verdant pastures below. You are my true shepherd and guide. Sometimes I stumble and fall, but your encouragement sustains me. The cup from which I poured out my wrath, you have filled to overflowing with your goodness. You have always been at my side, although I was too pre-occupied to notice. I am now regaining the strength to reach out and embrace you as you lead me out of my dark valley of worthlessness and self-pity to a new life.

Too long have I been buried deep in the dark valley of failure. I am grateful, Lord, for the courage you have given me to lift up my head and say: ''Thank you, God, for such a beautiful day.''

17
Giving Yourself

A couple who were friends of mine once asked me for advice concerning their troubled marriage. So one night we got together for a talk. After three intense hours I could hardly see and breathe. (They were chain smokers, and both the conversation and the evening were heated.)

I had given my all to help them sort out their difficulties and start living again. I felt that I had invested as much of myself as anyone could.

But the husband had built up a wall around himself, and that wall had not crumbled during our conversation. With a subtle smile meant to hide his insecurity, he reached for my hand and said: "Thank you for your time." I have never hit a man in my life, but I was seriously tempted to hit this man. Instead, I looked intently into his eyes and said: "I didn't give you my time; *I gave you myself.*"

Really, not until that moment did I understand the meaning of giving *myself*. I always thought that I was giving myself, but I was rather doing a job or just satisfying my own ego. Looking back, I discover that I rarely gave much of myself in my marriage. I gave my time, an interested look, a paycheck, a clean house, or a candy bar. But I never gave myself.

> I solemnly assure you, unless the grain of wheat falls to the earth and dies, it remains just a grain of wheat. But if it dies, it produces much fruit. The man who loves his life loses it, while the man who hates his life in this world preserves it to life eternal.
>
> *John 12:24-25*

Reflection

Dear Lord, I've always loved my life. I suppose that is why I've lost it. Now that I've learned that this life is only a testing ground, I'm beginning to store up some love and happiness for my eternal life in heaven.

When my marriage died, I died. I never thought that I could ever say this, but my divorce has made me a better person. Now I am a giving person, and what I give is myself.

Jesus, you always gave yourself to everyone you met. If you had given only your time or advice, you'd have lived longer. But because you gave yourself, your life ended on a cross. That is how you changed history, the world's and mine. Others before you uttered human wisdom. You spoke eternal truth.

"Know thyself" (Socrates).

"Control thyself" (Cicero).

"Give thyself" (Jesus).

18
God's Summons

God never called me to be successful,
God called me to be *faithful*.

Mother Teresa of Calcutta

Throughout my many years of schooling, I programed myself to succeed in whatever I did — from my first test in the primary grades to my first job promotion after graduating from college. I detest failing. I won't admit to failure.

But now I must concede that my marriage has failed. I have tried to hide this fact from others; I can no longer hide it from myself. Previously, when I stumbled as a marriage partner or as a parent, I would burn with the sensation that something was wrong with me. I was even afraid to glance at myself in a mirror, terrified at what I might see. I so desperately didn't want to hate myself then, and I don't want to hate myself now.

Reflection

Lord, *my* idea of a successful marriage was to have a home, kids, two cars, and a vacation every year. *Your* idea of success was that in acquiring all this I remain *faithful to myself.* You created me the way I am. I long to succeed in everything I do. I like clear-cut goals, and when my goal is "home" I want nothing to interfere with my prayers. But, dear God, it seems that I am lost these past few months. I'm not even sure where home is anymore.

I know now that I must be faithful to myself and to you. Only in this way can I build a new life that I can once again call "home."

Dear Lord, I have finally grown tall enough to see above and beyond the material things that surround and tend to overwhelm me at times. After my separation and during the divorce proceedings, all I could think of was money and how I was going to survive. Now I realize that it really doesn't matter whether I make fifteen thousand or thirty thousand dollars a year, drive a big or a compact car, live in the city or the suburbs. The only important matter is that I remain faithful — to you and to the person you created and nurtured me to be.

Lord, help me to persevere in my efforts to measure the success of my life by my fidelity to you and to your daily summons for me *to be me.*

19
Life in Focus

My line of work gives me the opportunity to visit many people in their homes. While traveling, I have uncovered a most disturbing fact. In almost every home that I visit, the TV is out of focus! Both adults and children seem not to be bothered by the distortion in their sets.

I've been tempted to say something, but I fear the response: "What business is it of yours?" People are either not aware of the fact or they just don't care. Possibly they can tolerate their TV being out of focus because their lives are just that — *out of focus*.

I often look at my life, not as it is, but as I want it to be. I spend much of my time finding out who I am *not*. I am not God, though sometimes I act like I am. I say, "I know, I know," when actually I don't know. I do know that I am not perfect. I'm really a C student, though I pretend to myself that I'm an A or a

B student. And now that my marriage has failed, I can see how much out of focus I have lived my own life. Oh, the mistakes I have made!

Reflection

Lord, let me count the ways you have shown your loving care for me:

I was broken and torn, and you healed me.

I was lost and alone, and you found me a home again.

I trembled long into the night, and you held me close.

I was blind, and you gave me a guiding hand.

I was spent, and you refreshed me.

I was at rope's end, and you showed me a new beginning.

Thank you, Lord, for helping me to place my life in proper focus.

20
Flying Free

One day as I was driving down the highway, a fly on the inside of my windshield distracted my attention from the road. Its constant buzzing, its incessant beating against the glass, soon became very annoying.

I tried everything to get rid of it. I opened the windows, turned on the defroster, and tried swatting it with a road map. But it always eluded me, finding some dashboard crevice in which to escape.

That fly had just come along for the ride, and it was my companion for many miles. Finally, however, while waiting at a stoplight, I managed to reach over and capture it with my two fingers. I was about ready to announce "Say hello to God" and snuff out its life, when I decided to grant it clemency. Rolling down my window, I let it fly free.

Reflection

Like that fly, Lord, I have been beating my head against the barriers that surround me on all sides. Every time I think I'm making progress, I hit another wall.

And like that fly, I've gone along for the ride. Lawyers, doctors, judges, priests, ministers, neighbors, in-laws — they have all talked to me, telling me what to do or what not to do. I've been so lost that I've heard hardly a word they have said. For months now I have been in a daze — walking around in a trance, collapsing into a state of shock. Like a beaten prize-fighter, I dread to hear the sound of the bell announcing the next round.

But now, Lord, you have given me a new life, a resurrection. Yes, the sun is shining again. The flowers are lovelier than ever. My new friends sincerely care about me. My old life was the only one that I knew; that is why I clung to it the way I did. At first, I did not like my new life. Gradually, however, it became tolerable and I began to like it. Now I love it!

I look back in disbelief to that period of my life when I seemed to be living in a totally dark room, knowing that there was a light switch on at least two of the walls and not being able to locate even one. Now I've thrown open the windows and pulled back the drapes on my new life. I'm still getting used to it, but I'm doing more than just taking oxygen. I'm smiling, joking, meeting new friends.

Lord, when you close one door, you always open other doors. You have clearly done this in my case. I, too, can fly free — now that the first door has been firmly closed.

The Beginning Experience

This experience is a weekend event for those who have lost a spouse through divorce or death. Presentations are given by a team of persons who have faced separation, divorce, or death in their own lives. Encountering yourself, working through the grief and the guilt, trusting again, deepening your relationship with God, and closing the door gently on the marriage are key topics on the weekend. There is time for reflection through writing. The twenty to thirty participants are also helped, through small-group sharing, to rediscover the joys of life and to pass through their grief to a new life.

For more information please write to:
THE BEGINNING EXPERIENCE
Central Office
3100 W. 41st Street
Sioux Falls, South Dakota 57105